6.99

First edition for the United States and Canada published in 2003 by Barron's Educational Series, Inc.

First edition for Great Britain published 2003 by Hodder Wayland, an imprint of Hodder Children's Books

Text © Pat Thomas 2003
Illustrations © Lesley Harker 2003

*All inquiries should be addressed to:*
Barron's Educational Series, Inc.
250 Wireless Boulevard
Hauppauge, NY 11788
***http://www.barronseduc.com***

Library of Congress Catalog Card No. 2002111584

ISBN-13 : 978-0-7641-2461-7
ISBN-10 : 0-7641-2461-7

Printed in China
9 8 7 6 5 4

# My New Family

## A FIRST LOOK AT ADOPTION

PAT THOMAS
ILLUSTRATED BY LESLEY HARKER

BARRON'S

You live in a very
special family.

You needed a family and your parents needed a child to love and care for. They wanted you to be a part of their family.

There are lots of ways to make a family.

Sometimes children live with their birth parents – the ones who gave birth to them.

Sometimes they live with relatives or other people who are not their parents.

And, sometimes children are adopted into a completely new family.

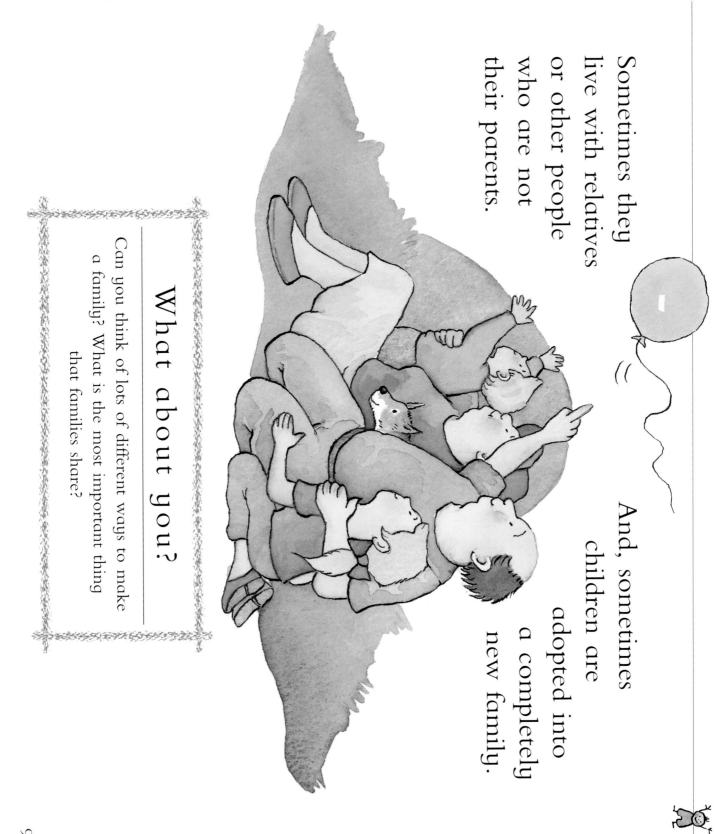

## What about you?

Can you think of lots of different ways to make a family? What is the most important thing that families share?

We all have birth parents.

But sometimes our birth parents cannot look after us as well as they would like to.

When this happens, a child sometimes goes to live with a foster family or stays in a children's home.

A foster family or a children's home usually looks after a child for only a little while, until the parents are able to take care of their child again.

But sometimes parents
just cannot look
after their children.

When this
happens, the
children may
stay with a foster
family until a
new family can
be found. This
new family is
their adoptive
family.

Every year lots of children all over the world are adopted – sometimes as babies and sometimes as older children.

When children are adopted, they go to live with another family forever.

Adopting a child is not always easy. Grown-ups who want to adopt often have to answer a lot of questions about who they are and how they live.

Sometimes parents and children have to wait a long time before they can be part of a new family.

15

When your adoptive parents first saw you, they knew you were meant to be a part of their family.

When they were finally able to adopt you, they made a promise to love you and take care of you forever. They looked forward to watching you grow and teaching you new things.

Sometimes adopted children look like the members of their new family. Sometimes they may come from a different part of the country or another part of the world.

But the way we look and where we come from are not the most important things in a family. What is important is sharing some of the same interests and learning to understand and love each other, whatever happens.

Some children who were adopted think they are different or second best — even though this is not true.

They may also feel confused or angry about not knowing much about their birth parents.

This is normal and your parents understand this. Talking to them about how you are feeling can help them understand when you feel sad.

Sometimes it can make you feel sad when you think about your birth parents. You might not understand why they had you adopted.

Sometimes adoptive parents do not know much about your birth parents. Whatever they know they will try to share with you when they can.

## What about you?

What do your adoptive parents know about your birth parents?
Is there anything that you would like to know?
Can your parents help you to find out more?
Look at pages 28-29.

Remember that both of your sets of parents have given you something special. Your birth parents gave you life.

Your adoptive parents gave you a home and family and the love you need to grow up healthy and happy.

There are many different kinds of families. But there are some things that make all families the same.

One thing is the way they always try to love and support one another — just like everyone in your family does.

# HOW TO USE THIS BOOK

Many adoptive parents agonize over the question, "What do we tell the children?" What to say and when to say it are difficult decisions to make. Much depends on your child's age, sensitivity, and level of understanding. It is generally accepted that children should know they are adopted even before they fully understand what it means. As soon as possible, initiate conversations about adoption. Try to make talk about adoption a part of normal everyday conversation. You might say, for example: "Before we adopted you we lived in New York City, but now we live in Westchester." Casually dropping the subject in the conversation like this lets children know that it is OK to talk about it when they want to. If adoption becomes part of the language of the family, it will not seem like such a big deal when the time comes to discuss it in depth.

Before you begin to talk to your child about adoption, practice what you want to say. Make sure you are prepared to answer any questions that come up. Books like this are helpful for getting a discussion going and are supposed to be read more than once.

Give yourself some credit. Adopting a child is a major life journey. Adoptive parents sometimes suffer from "super parent" syndrome. They may feel that they have something to prove to others about how competent they are. Try to let this go because it gets in the way of open communication. You have come far enough to want to talk to your child about it. Let your loving feelings for your child be your guide about the best way to do this.

Talk to your children about all the different types of families. There are divorced families that include stepparents and siblings. Some children live with relatives other than their parents or with foster families. Schools can make a similar effort. Whether there are adopted children in the class or not, discussions about family should always include information on different types of families so that all the children understand that there is nothing wrong with being adopted.

Children love to hear their own stories. Very young children may only want to know pieces of the story, for instance how you came to get them the day they were adopted. As they get older they will ask more questions. Create an environment where it's OK for your child to ask questions. Keep all the information you have on your child's background in a safe place. When the time comes, it will make it easier to answer questions.

Many parents put together a book for their adopted children. They collect pictures and stories, and their child can add more later. Make your child's "life story book" using whatever you have – pictures of your family and of the birth family, if available. Other ideas might be photographs of previous homes or pets. If information is lacking (perhaps as a result of a closed adoption), you must do what you can with what you've got so your child has something to build on.

There are many myths about adoption that linger from the past. Though the adoption process has changed a great deal in the past twenty years, adoption can still be presented in a negative way. We still hear comments like: "Your parents didn't want you" or "We couldn't have any children of our own." Similarly it is easy for adopted children to feel they are somehow "second best." In this book, the author has attempted to introduce the subject from a more positive angle, and encourages parents to avoid making children feel grateful for being adopted.

Reassure your child that she didn't do anything wrong, and the break-up of her birth family was not her fault. Adoption is usually an act of love on the part of a birth parent. Help your child to understand the impossible position her parents might have been in when they had her adopted. Stress that adoption seemed the only way that her birth parents thought they could help her. By making an adoption plan, they believed that they were giving their child the best opportunity for a happy life, with a loving family who could look after her properly. When stuck for an explanation, always err on the side of love.

Acknowledge your child's feelings and answer all questions, even if they are difficult. If you don't know the answer to a particular question, say so.

Celebrate your child's adoption day as well as his birthday. This can be a celebration involving the whole family. Special adoption celebration cards are also now available.

Use your adoption agency. If necessary, they will give you advice and help you to seek out more background information about your adopted child.

# GLOSSARY

**adoption**  When a child goes to live with another family forever. When a child is adopted, the adoptive parents have a legal responsibility to look after that child.

**birth parents**  The people who created you with their bodies and helped give you life.

**foster family**  A family who looks after a child for a short while, for instance when the child's birth parents are very ill. When the birth parents are able to look after the child, he or she goes back to live with them.

# FURTHER READING

*Adoption Is for Always*
by Linda Walvoord Girard
(Albert Whitman & Co, 1991)

*How I Was Adopted*
by Joanna Cole (William Morrow & Co., 1999)

*A Mother for Choco*
by Keiko Kasza (G. P. Putnam's Sons, 1992)

*The Mulberry Bird: An Adoption Story*
by Anne Braff Brodzinsky (Perspectives Press, 1996)

*Tell Me Again About the Night I Was Born*
by Jamie Lee Curtis (HarperCollins, 1996)

*Why Was I Adopted?*
by Carole Livingson
(Carol Publishing Group, 1997)

# RESOURCES

*Adoptive Families*
New Hope Communications LLC
2472 Broadway
New York, NY 10024
To subscribe: Phone (800) 372-3300; Fax: (212) 877-9198
e-mail: Info@adoptivefam.org
http://www.adoptivefamilies.com/

*Adoptive Parent Support Groups*
http://www.adoptivefamilies.com/support_group.php

*The world's largest circulation, most detailed and inclusive magazine on adoptive parenting issues; informative website. Find an adoption support group in your area on the Adoptive Families magazine website.*

*Celebrate Adoption, Inc.*
P.O. Box 4405
Bennington, VT 05201-4405
http://www.celebrateadoption.org

*A nonprofit organization aimed at advancing a positive image of adoption through public awareness, education, and media advocacy.*

*About Adoption*
http://www.adoption.about.com/

*Adoption.com*
www.adoption.com

*News, links, information, and more, related to adoption issues, adoptive parenting, and adoption-related services.*

*Adoption Learning Partners*
http://www.adoptionlearningpartners.org/

*Provides e-learning courses for all members of the adoption circle with the goal of advancing adoption through education.*